CW01643329

Best wishes

Betty Carter

Betty Carter

20th CENTURY GIRL
and other stories

Published by

MELROSE BOOKS

An Imprint of Melrose Press Limited
St Thomas Place, Ely
Cambridgeshire
CB7 4GG, UK
www.melrosebooks.com

FIRST EDITION

Cover designed by Jeremy Kay

ISBN 978 1 906561 60 4

Printed and bound in Great Britain by:
CPI Antony Rowe. Chippenham, Wiltshire

FSC
Mixed Sources
Product group from well-managed forests and other controlled sources
Cert no. SGS-COC-2953
www.fsc.org
© 1996 Forest Stewardship Council

Foreword

Betty Carter grew up in what is now known as the West Midlands, and I had the good fortune to meet her when I moved there after my marriage over fifty years ago. Originally she was my work colleague, both of us working in a physiotherapy department together, but she soon showed her true self and became a very good friend indeed. I also helped when she had her private physiotherapy practice, so we have seen a lot of 'life' together; some of it quite serious, but Betty also has a keen sense of humour, so we had fun and many laughs with each other.

Life has not always been easy – as it rarely is – but she never seemed to lose her love of life and her sense of humour.

She has always been a great reader, and in my early days I used to be given a list of authors that she recommended I should read, so my repertoire increased enormously.

Betty lives with her husband not very far from where she was brought up, and she remains what I can only describe as a close, life-long friend.

Dorothy M. Forster, B.Sc., MCSP

Contents

Twentieth-Century Girl

Oh my, looking back over the years, I cannot imagine I was born in 1923 – over eighty-five years ago, and what a different world it was then.

My mother and father met as Sunday School teachers in about 1915. My father, after seeing Rosie come into church every Sunday morning with her father, vowed, "That is the girl I shall marry!"

In 1917 he joined the army, after having signed up in 1915 and being left on the reserve list until 1917. He joined the Royal Engineers with just a year to finalise his apprenticeship as a railway engineer with the Great Western Railway. He was sent to Borden Training Camp and when ready his battalion was to be sent to Russia, as the Revolution there had broken out in 1917. Just before embarking, the military powers that be asked if there were any of the troops trained in railway engineering. My father put up his hand with another recruit. The rest of the battalion went to Russia and not one of them returned; they were all killed.

My father and his comrade-in-arms were sent to Salonika in Greece to help restore the rolling stock which needed immediate attention after the Germans had retreated. The Greeks always bought British rolling stock.

Mr Popadopalos, the manager in Salonika, had a

Scottish wife and every Sunday my father was invited to lunch.

He had found wandering in the camp a beautiful blonde Great Dane. She was starving, so he fed her, and she always slept under his bed. When he left Salonika in 1920 to return to the UK, 'Baby', the Dane, was taken in by the Popadopalos family. They had tried very hard to persuade my father to stay in Greece but he wanted to return to his Rosie. They were married in June 1921, and when my grandmother died the following August they stayed to keep house for my grandfather at Lea House, Albrighton in Shropshire.

In 1923 my grandfather remarried, so Rosie and Harold had to find a house of their own, which they quickly managed to do. I was born a few weeks later.

I spent many happy holidays at my grandfather's house, a small farm called Lea Manor. There my love of dogs began. There were three – Rex, a large Springer Spaniel; Major, a Roan Spaniel; and Dido, a beautiful Dalmatian, who hurt my legs with her large waving tail.

At five years old, I was sent to a small prep school which I loved – had lots of friends and adored the headmistress. "Always, girls, remember your deportment and always wear your hat and gloves."

At the age of 7, after passing the entrance exam, I was sent to the local girls' high school. It broke my heart to leave Ely House College, my prep school, but, as my mother explained, "You are an only child, you need to mix with lots of girls and you will get a better education if you want to go to university or enter the professions." She was quite right, of course, and except for a few hiccups with one form mistress, who didn't like me very much and gave me an acute inferiority complex, I settled in a very good school and stayed until I was 18, in 1941.

The war had been raging for two years!

My choice of career was to train as a Chartered Physiotherapist. I was successful in being admitted to a training school at the Queen Elizabeth Hospital in

Birmingham. Due to the bombing, I wasn't allowed to 'dig' in Birmingham, so had to travel sixty miles each day, arriving in the early morning and stepping out of Snowhill Station into Colmore Row, full of rubble and burst water mains after bombing raids the night before. After three months we were sent to various hospital departments, treating civilians and military patients.

The military patients were the result of terrible injuries sustained at Dunkirk, and later many who were shipped home from the North Africa Campaign. Their stoicism and bravery in dealing so young with such dreadful injuries was just incredible.

When the Canadians arrived in England they were very anxious to play their part in the action. After some time they managed to persuade Mr Churchill to send them on a mission and he sent them to a place called Dieppe on the French coast. It was a complete disaster; the Germans were waiting for them and inflicted many deaths and injuries. Some of the wounded came to QE and I was sent to treat a young boy of 18. He was physically uninjured but was suffering from total shell shock, which caused paralysis of his legs. Many of my family were in Canada, including my grandfather, aunt and cousins, so I was able to communicate with him to a certain extent. It was just awful to see him fighting to recover, every inch of the way. One morning when I went to the ward he wasn't there. He had been shipped home, so I never heard the outcome of his story.

During this time, our wards were full of civilians critically injured in the bombing of Birmingham. One dear old lady, I shall never forget, came to our department as an outpatient. She was well into her seventies, dressed in her Sunday best; Edwardian hat, long navy coat and button boots. She had lived in a small street of terraced houses which had been bombed with oil bombs. She had her life but all that remained of her hands was, on the left, a stump of a thumb, no other fingers; on her right no thumb, a stump of index finger and a little finger. Her courage and bravery were simply awe-inspiring.

There were many, many casualties. Ansell's Brewery gave up their cellarage for use as a medical distribution centre. It was manned mostly by medical students. An ambulance used to arrive in the courtyard of the old General Hospital after an alert at night. It picked up three medical students and two physios with a pot of Quink ink, a fountain pen and a register. That was our job, to register the casualties as they were brought in. Very tricky! One night when a bomb was dropped in the courtyard of the hospital one of our more volatile physios was heard for many miles when she nearly fell into the crater!

I cannot convey more strongly, in spite of the tragedies, that there was always laughter and fun and a great determination that we were going to win this war, whatever happened to us. In 1944 I was on the train going to hospital when I saw dozens of planes flying south for the invasion. We, of course, didn't know this at the time but it was an awesome sight.

We had all lost loved ones. My dear cousin Norman was a tank commander with the 5th Army in Italy. He had travelled the length of Italy, which, as we now know, was terrible fighting. On the outskirts of Florence at the last stand with the Germans falling back, he was killed by a sniper and is now buried in the military cemetery on the Coriano Ridge. He was like a brother to me and I still miss him very much. He was 24, married, with a 6-week-old baby girl, Diana.

Many of my friends were bomber pilots, flying Lancasters and Wellingtons. Many were killed in bombing raids over Germany. Many made it home without undercarriages and completely shot to pieces only to belly crash at their aerodromes and blow up.

My one dear friend died from his injuries when a Canadian pilot he was instructing to pilot his Wellington bomber crashed into the trees at Didcot Aerodrome. His brother was an engineer on a T-class submarine and after being depth charged at the bottom of the English Channel, he finally after ten days managed to refloat the sub. After some leave, he was sent to the Mediterranean and died when HMS *Tigris* was blown up while attacking the Italian navy in Naples harbour. There is a plaque on the Embankment in London to HMS *Tigris*.

Taking our final exams was quite difficult. During the written finals the air raid warnings rang out. No one took any notice, just carried on writing. We had to go to London to Guy's Examinations Hall for our vivas which were rather long, 2–3 hours sometimes. I was very lucky. I managed to stay with friends in Ealing and never once did we have air raid warnings. Very lucky, as the doodlebugs were becoming a great nuisance and a danger.

After qualifying in 1943 I stayed at the General for a further year and then transferred to an emergency military hospital in Dudley – 'The Guest'. I stayed there until 1961 in full-time and part-time capacities. In 1951 I had become a partner in a private practice and went on working until 1981. I absolutely loved my life as a physiotherapist. I don't really know what other career I could have done.

It is very interesting to look back and see how things have changed … I loved the music of the thirties and forties – Henry Hall, Jack Payne, Jack Hylton, etc. I also love classical music and was lucky enough to go with my parents to many concerts at our local civic hall. During this time, the Halle Orchestra, the Beecham Orchestra, the Liverpool Philharmonic and a number of others came to give wonderful concerts. After my parents died, a friend and I went together; she had also lost her parents … I remember very well Sir John Barbirolli, conductor of the Halle, when he was getting rather older, leaving the rostrum and being met by an assistant with a small shawl to put over his shoulders. I used to promenade during the war years for 2s 6d to see the Halle and a young, dark-haired Sir John and his wonderful orchestra.

In 1943, after qualifying, I rejoined the small dramatic society started by my friend John Denton. He put on plays for the Red Cross. During my student days, I just didn't have the time for play-acting but I was so delighted to rejoin in 1943 and by this time we were producing plays, such as *Hay Fever*, in a church hall. We were called 'The Yewland Players'.

In September 1943 I went for a rehearsal at John's home. He announced the arrival of a new member – a very handsome policeman from our local village. Our eyes met as he entered John's lounge; that was it! He left the police force in December 1945 and applied for training as a school teacher. We got engaged. During the war, he had been detailed to the bombing of Birmingham and Coventry.

He took himself to a small Church of England college, St John's in Ystrad Meurig in Wales, whilst he was waiting for a place in teacher training college. St John's was run by two Church of England parsons, both with a BA from Oxford University. St John's had quite a few ex RAF, Army and Navy officers waiting to go to Lampeter College to become parsons.

In 1947 Teddy went to Burderop Park Emergency College in Wiltshire. It was very hard as the winter was one of the worst for years, solid icicles, and snow swept the Downs – very little food.

In March 1948 he passed out with a teaching certificate and we were married on the thirty-first.

Later on Teddy was accepted into Gray's Inn of Court and trained as a barrister for three years. It was hard for him as an external student and still working in teaching. During the time of his teaching career, he obtained an extra diploma from Birmingham Training College and joined the Remedial Team, teaching children with learning difficulties to read.

He retired from teaching in 1973 and became a model with a Birmingham agency, working all over England for various photographers for advertisements of various products and also well-known building firms.

In 1951, as I have already stated, I joined a girl in a private practice – actually the first in my hometown, Wolverhampton – now there are many. We worked with orthopaedic surgeons and shared rooms, which was a very good working relationship. We also visited patients near and far in their homes; it was very pleasant to get away from the surgery for a spell.

In 1981 we sold the practice to two young, enthusiastic physios. My partner retired completely. I continued in a dental practice and a private hospital, treating outpatients by electrolysis for Hirsutes.

In 1980 my father died, of a broken heart, I always felt. He was 82 years old. My mother had been ill with Alzheimer's from 1971, gradually getting worse, and finally, after my father and I had looked after her, she went into a nursing home. She died in 1981, aged 85 years.

I finally gave up practising when I was 75 years old – dedicated – perhaps?

My husband and I travelled widely – mostly cruising, whilst we were working; saving every penny to cure our wanderlust. My husband has survived two nasty accidents; breaking his femur and having an artificial prosthesis replacing his hip joint, falling backwards downstairs, and being taught to walk again in hospital. He is now 95 years old and rather frail but fortunately has all his marbles. I have trouble with my eyesight and am no longer able to drive long distances, which has restricted our outings and holidays – but we are still together into the twenty-first century, which is so wonderful although living rather a restricted life. Heigh-ho – may it long continue!

A Norfolk Incident

John and Elizabeth Carter decided that, this year, they would not travel abroad for their holidays, but visit Norfolk and travel the Broads by car rather than by boat.

John, who was very clever at arranging vacations, found a hotel which had been a large Queen Anne house with a beautiful garden sloping down to the river. The house had originally belonged to an elderly gentleman who was very keen on astronomy. He had added onto the roof of the house a tower. In this tower he kept his very large telescope. He spent hours in the early 1800s gazing at the stars, hoping against hope to find a new galaxy.

The journey down from the Midlands, where the Carters lived, in a tiny village with two large greens, was uneventful. They arrived in the afternoon of the first Saturday of their holiday and were shown to a delightful bedroom on the first floor.

The bedroom, with another room next door, had obviously been one. Quite clearly it could have been the drawing room. Long windows stretched from floor to ceiling with beautiful trailing wisteria peeping through the panes.

After unpacking and settling in, they went downstairs to the bar for a drink before dinner. Dinner was very good, and after coffee and a short walk by the river they retired to bed, feeling very relaxed and rather tired.

Next day they drove to the nearest village, had lunch at a very old inn and returned to the hotel. They sat on the terrace until dinner time, reading and admiring the view over the garden and watching the many craft cruising up and down the river, and watched with admiration the skill with which the boats were 'parked'. After dinner they retired quite early.

After falling into a deep sleep, Elizabeth was fully awakened by strange sounds all round her bed. She glanced at her bedside clock; it was one o'clock. The sounds were very pleasant – girlish laughter, silks and satins rustling, as the girls chased one another round the room and round the bed.

Elizabeth steeled herself and got out of her bed. All sounds and rustles instantly stopped. She put her ear to the bedroom wall and listened – not a sound! She looked through the windows – nothing, absolutely no one about.

She returned to her bed. The sounds returned, and continued for another hour.

This sequence of events continued, every night: Monday, Tuesday and Wednesday. All this time John had been fast asleep, every night.

On Thursday morning Elizabeth came to a decision. At breakfast she said to John, "Have you heard any strange sounds in the hotel?"

"Oh," he said, "I wondered when you might say something. I have been trying to find some answers." Apparently he had been pestering the management and got absolutely nowhere.

They decided to visit the library in Norwich to inquire into the history of the families who had lived there. High up on the wall of the library, opposite the entrance, was a large oil painting of the house. Unfortunately they were unsuccessful in finding any of the information they required. They really hadn't the time for the staff to find data. Their time was limited as they were moving next morning to Cromer.

So – the mystery was unsolved.

John told Elizabeth his experience a few days later when they were relaxing in the sunshine, experiences which were supported by what Elizabeth told him. On the first Sunday morning, at breakfast, they were glancing through their newspapers when a voice whispered in his ear. The words were undecipherable to him. He looked up, thinking Elizabeth had spoken to him, but she was reading and had obviously not said a word. Their table was directly underneath their bedroom. The 'whisperings' had continued every morning for the rest of their stay. Nothing more could be said or done. Final.

Moonstone Cottage

Mary Moonshine had lived in the seventeenth-century cottage all her life. She looked out through the latticed windows, down the garden path to the lychgate, which led into the lane and hence to the main Dartmouth road.

Moonstone Cottage was situated in a small valley on the edge of Dartmoor. In spring, the garden was full of daffodils, tulips, hyacinths and masses of bluebells; in summer, sweet-smelling roses of every kind, delphiniums, lupins and many others, right through to autumn.

Mary sat in warmer weather with the windows wide open to let in the heavenly scents which pervaded the air. Coffee on a small table by her side, she said a little prayer of thankfulness for living in such beautiful surroundings. She was now in her mid-sixties and felt she must think and plan for the future. Where to go when things got more difficult?

Dartmouth was her choice, in a few years' time. A nice flat overlooking the river would be just marvellous for her. Her Roan Spaniel Max was now 10 years old, so no hurry for a few years yet.

Oggy Anderson came every week, to look after the garden, cut the grass, etc. He arrived in a very ancient van which seemed to go on for ever. He kept her well supplied with logs for her wood-burning stove, so all in all everything was hunky-dory on the home front. Her own little Morris Mini was still adequate for her short journeys shopping, treats on the moor and into surrounding villages.

Summer had really arrived. On a hot June day with hardly a cloud in the sky, Mary, as usual, was in her sitting room, coffee by her side after partaking of a very tasty dinner. Everywhere was quite still, until suddenly she heard voices. Apprehensively she arose, and went through the dining room to the kitchen. The latter had been the byre, housing the cows and sheep.

A conversation was taking place between several people, one or two males, and there were the sounds of children chattering and playing and women's voices, all talking in a very strong Devonshire dialect. The talk was about everyday happenings. When haymaking should begin, and how many people should be asked to help; and the supply and cooking of food.

Mary stood in the doorway, transfixed and frightened to move. There were no figures or misty hazes, absolutely nothing whatsoever to see. Gradually the voices faded away and disappeared altogether. She made her way slowly back to the sitting room and collapsed, trembling, into her chair. This 'happening' continued every evening around eight o'clock and lasted about ten minutes. Nothing else occurred at any time during the day or night.

Mary told no one of her dilemma, but finally decided to tape-record the events and was astounded to hear the voices quite clearly. The happenings were not frightening in any way and became quite a part of her life. She couldn't decide which century they were living in but it could easily have been the sixteenth or seventeenth.

Three weeks after the voices first started Mary's cousin, Molly Moonshine, was due for her annual three weeks' holiday. Mary looked forward every year to this visit and planned outings to various parts of Devon, picnics on the moor and, of course, to Dartmouth with a trip up the river. Molly duly arrived, very like Mary in stature and character. They had always 'got on' particularly well, being the same age, within a few months.

After Molly had been there for around ten days Mary decided to tell her of her voices. Nothing had happened since Molly arrived, so, in apprehension, she raised the matter after dinner one evening. She told Molly a little about the occurrences, and switched on the tape. Nothing! Absolutely nothing! The tape was completely blank. She tried several times but no sound came forth.

Molly asked for further information. She was amazed, intrigued and rather nervous about it all. Every night for the rest of her holiday the two cousins sat with their coffee, talked, and tried the tape again and again – still nothing! She pleaded with Mary to apply for more experienced help.

After Molly's departure Mary ate her evening meal, and over her coffee she switched on the tape at eight o'clock on the dot when the voices started again in the kitchen. They were recorded and played back many times, perfectly satisfactorily.

Two days later Mary made an appointment and went to see the vicar, the Rev. John Baxter, hoping he would be sympathetic, which he was. The next evening around 7.30 p.m. he arrived. The tape was switched on – it was blank.

The vicar donned his clerical robes, took his beautiful hand cross from its case and walked into the kitchen. He spent some time there, chanting, praying for the spirits which were haunting to depart with God.

At the end of this time, he bowed his head and was aware of beings all around him; strange scents and aromas filled the atmosphere then gradually began to fade silently away and he was left in complete stillness, alone. He returned to the sitting room and Mary. He sat down in complete exhaustion. After two days he returned to Moonstone Cottage. He had spent his time going through all the old church records. Over the centuries many families had lived at Moonstone Cottage and farmed the smallholding. One family from the eighteenth century seemed to stand out to him. A family consisting of the elderly grandmother, her son and his wife, three children, a boy of 14 years and two girls aged 12 and 10. Also a brother-in-law around 30 years old, whose wife had died in childbirth, and the baby. Their name was Godsbright.

Many Godsbrights had lived at Moonstone, the farm gaining in acreage, cattle, sheep and three or four large fields where barley and wheat were grown. In the late 1700s, a dreadful disease struck the crops; in addition there was a drought and the fields became a desert.

The Godsbrights never seemed to recover from this tragedy. A year later, tragedy struck again. All their stock either died or had to be slaughtered. The land was sold to a neighbouring farmer and Moonstone Cottage itself was sold to strangers. The family left the area and no one had any idea where they went.

Obviously their spirits had returned to the place where they were happiest.

Sadness completely overwhelmed Mary. She decided that she must go away on holiday to forget the tragedy of the lovely Godsbright family. When she returned she would seriously think of moving to Dartmouth. Perhaps she might be able to find a flat or bungalow especially where she could take dear old Maxie. Who knows, perhaps the Godsbrights would help from their cottage in the sky … named Sunstone.

The Butelier Family

Marie Doreena Butelier was actually born in Ireland. She was the only daughter of William Charles Butelier, living south of Dublin, in County Cork. The Butelier family had originated in France. They were wine stewards. Marie's particular branch of the family had joined the household of one William, who was to become 'William the Conqueror'.

His ancestor, also William Charles, joined the court and gradually rose from 'pot boy' to head steward, hence the name Butelier. He arrived in Britain in 1066 with the invasion army. He stayed with King William for many years, but then decided to chance his luck farther afield. King William gave him an estate in Devon. He built a small castle with twin towers.

When Marie Doreena was born, there were many branches of the original family spreading all over Britain and into Ireland. The year was 1432. Marie's mother and father both drowned whilst travelling in a small fishing boat to visit friends farther down the coastline. A sudden squall meant they had no chance when their craft overturned. It was decided that Marie should go and live with her paternal grandmother, in Britain.

She arrived on a bleak day in early March with her old nurse as her only companion. Grandmère's house was a large manor built on the site of a ruined castle. In fact most of the outside walls were the original castle walls. The manor was in Devon, on the edge of a large desolate and dangerous moor.

She was welcomed into loving arms as many of her aunts, uncles and cousins still lived there. She was given a spacious, beautiful room overlooking the garden. Her bed was large with lovely draperies and very comfortable-looking pillows and bed linen. Her nurse had a truckle bed in the corner of the room. Her dressing table was oak, with draperies to match the curtains and her bed. Marie was just 11 years old when she arrived at Grandmère Butelier's manor and she was to stay many years until she was old enough to marry, which in the 1400s was usually 15 or 16 years, but in the meantime strange things began to happen.

Marie spent much of her time reading, sitting on the cushioned window seat in her room. From time to time she thought she heard a baby laughing and sometimes crying. She made enquiries but was told there wasn't a baby in the house. She completely believed what she was told. All her cousins were her age group, or older.

One particular afternoon she heard the laughter again. This time it seemed closer, so going out of her room and looking along the corridor, she espied a small girl of about six years dancing and laughing away from her and disappearing along the corridor on the left which led to the servants' quarters. She followed; the child had completely disappeared, was nowhere to be seen. She continued on to the end room of the corridor where the sewing woman worked. She entered the room – it was quite empty except for a table with sewing implements and in the corner a spinning wheel – the wheel was slowly turning and as she gazed, it stopped. She went back to her room very puzzled.

The same occurrence happened many times until the day she ventured out into the corridor once again. The child was coming towards her this time, singing and dancing happily along. When the child was a few yards from Marie she smiled at her and turned into the old castle wall and disappeared. As you can imagine, Marie was stunned, completely amazed but certainly not afraid.

For quite a few months nothing happened. In the meantime she decided to speak to one of her uncles of whom she was rather fond. He too was completely amazed and totally believed her story. He decided the best thing to do was to go down into the vaults where all the important papers for the family and household were kept. Marie accompanied him and painstakingly they went through decades of history of the Butelier family. After days of poring over papers they came to a bunch of yellowed parchments, tied with a red ribbon, a history of the time of 1230. There were just two families living in the castle. It had apparently only become a ruin in about 1350, after years of being unoccupied.

One family was old and hadn't any children. The other family had one small girl aged six years, called Marianne. Marianne was a very happy little girl – skipping, dancing and singing all over the castle, round and round the gardens and in the wood which surrounded the castle – thick with bluebells and snowdrops in springtime.

One day Marianne decided to climb the winding, worn, rickety stairs up to the tower in the west wing. She arrived on the flat roof, still dancing and skipping around, when a sudden large gust of wind lifted her high in the air and dropped her like a snowflake, down and down to the ground beneath. The gardener that day had dug a large bed in which to plant roses and summer flowers, hence there was a tall pile of soft earth at the side of the hole. Marianne landed on the pile of earth but by the time she was found she was quite dead. She was buried in her tiny beech coffin in the rose bed, and until the day Marie and her uncle read of this they both knew the rose bed was still there, blooming with beautiful flowers.

Marie was inconsolable for many days but finally realised she had seen Marianne for the last time. When she felt a little better she went to the wood and gathered wild flowers and took them to the small chapel attached to the manor but also a part of the old castle. She laid the flowers on the altar, said a little prayer for Marianne and returned to her room. She went every day with fresh flowers but the ones she placed on the small altar never faded, they remained always fresh and beautiful.

Marie grew up, married a neighbour's son and went to live in her own manor house nearby. She never forgot Marianne and even as an old lady visited the tiny chapel in the Butelier manor. She died aged 72 years in 1504, a great-grandmother. Her children told of her last word when she was dying: Marianne. As she died a beautiful smile hovered around her lips and she breathed a great sigh.

As a member of the modern Butelier family, now known as 'Butler', I am especially interested in this wide-flung family. Butlers are in America, Canada, all over the world, in fact but still known as Butelier in France. As my ophthalmic surgeon who is 'pure' Irish from Dublin tells me, "You are pure Norman!"

Heigh-ho, it's a funny world!

My branches of the Butler family were brewers, brewing good old English ale for the stolid, good old English working man – but they did emigrate from County Cork in the late 1700s. As my friends say to me: "You are the result of the Potato Famine," – pity, I like potatoes. Ah me!

Sir Thomas Tittlemouse, MBME

(Member of the British Mouse Empire)

Sir Thomas Tittlemouse refused to be called Tommy (so lowering to prestige, he would remark) and glowered with all his mousehood to anyone who presumed.

He lived in a great Baronial Manor Hall. The main entrance was in a very tall bank. He had several side entrances, "For the trades' people, don't you know?"!

He was a very wise and intelligent mouse; many people rang for appointments, and many just called for advice. He had advice for them on many subjects – money, ancestry, trade – almost anything mice required to know.

He had a wife – she was number two. His first had died in childbirth with their first litter – twelve – most of them had died – just two or three survived. All grown up now with families of their own and grand-mice. Most came for Christmas and he was always pleased when they went. Their noise drove him mad.

Second wifey was flirtatious and very pretty – lovely eyes and shining fur. He had to keep a strict eye upon her, for her own sake.

One day just before Christmas, a stranger arrived at the main entrance and was quickly told to go around to the 'Trades'. He was a very large mouse with black fur, black as his eyes, which had an evil glint in them. He came with some 'cock and bull' story, and no one could make out what he was saying, as his grammar and speech were so awful.

Sir Thomas's private secretary did his best, so did his valet, but to no avail. The stranger was asked to leave. His protests were loud and ugly – he had to be restrained by Sir Thomas's two bodyguards – also large black-furred mice. He was finally thrown out of the Hall, but before the final thrust he espied Lady Tilly Tittlemouse gazing over the banisters at him, goggle-eyed and amazed. He gave her a broad wink and disappeared. But did he? No, he did not. He skulked around the undergrowth on the bank, watching the activities and goings on at the Hall.

He noted Lady Tittlemouse sallied forth every afternoon around 3 p.m. with her personal maid to visit friends for tea and crumpets. He awaited his opportunity and one afternoon crept up behind the two ladies, knocked the maid on the head and slung her into oblivion. He rode off pronto with Lady T, with a large paw over her mouth to stop her screaming and flinging her over his shoulder, making off rapidly to his nest. The latter was a filthy, dank, tumbledown nest under a large drainage pipe, which gurgled and hissed every few minutes with the flow of water.

He slunk into his abode and threw Lady T onto his filthy, flea-ridden bed and tied her down with twine from the coarse grass in the field outside, stuffing more of the grass into her screaming mouth.

Living nearby was Bobby Mouse. He lived in a very clean, delightful bungalow nest, quite twenty feet from the Black Devil, as he called him.

Bobby constantly spied on him because not only did he not trust him, he was also rather scared of him.

This particular day he was doing his spring cleaning. He was making rather a good job of it as he was thinking whether to move or not, as the Black Devil was getting more and more aggressive and he was aware of strangers visiting him with strange packets in their bags. Obviously drugs, he thought. One had fallen out one day so he picked it up and was about to take it to Mickey the local police mouse.

He espied the Black Devil with his struggling bundle, and after they entered his abode he crept up and peeped through the filthy dirty window. What he saw horrified him, so he sped off immediately at great pace to the police. PC Mickey was just cleaning his windows but very quickly listened to what Bobby had to say and called up his police reserves. In minutes they arrived and set off for the Black Devil's abode. They stoned and broke down the door, seized the Black Devil and transported him back to the police station.

After attending to Lady T, Bobby escorted her to his bungalow. He gave her a large cup of sweet tea and a cherry bun and phoned Sir Thomas.

Sir Thomas's muscle man arrived at Bobby's home and escorted Lady T and Bobby back to the Hall. On their way they found Matilda Mouse, Lady T's maid, who by that time was recovering on a stone bench, shivering and with a large black eye.

Sir Thomas was overjoyed to see Lady T and Matilda and immediately ordered a large meal for them, and Bobby was invited to stay for a few days.

An Alphabet of Animals, Birds and Fish For Children

a) Archie the Ant

b) Boris the Bullfrog

c) Cuthbert the Cuckoo

d) Danny the Dragon

e) Ellie the Elephant

f) Fanny the Finch

g) Gilbert the Gander

h) Harry the Hippo

i) Isadore the Iguana

j) Johnny the Jackdaw

k) Katie the Kingfisher

l) Lawrence the Lion

m) Maisie the Minnie Mouse

n) Norman the Nuthatch

o) Oswald the Owl

p) Percy the Pike

q) Queeny the Quail

r) Reggie the Rat

s) Sidney the Snail

t) Tommy the Tortoise

u) Unwin the Unicorn

v) Violet the Vixen

w) Wally the Walrus

x) Xavier the Xyphoid

y) Yolande the Yeti

z) Zoa the Zebra

ARCHIE THE ANT

Archie the Ant heaved a great sigh,
As he crawled under his favourite stone,
He was tired and wet, and fed up with himself,
My, was he glad to be home.

Archie the Ant had a friend called Antoine,
Who hailed from the land of the sun,
He was handsome and bold, full of great charm,
A dashing young man, full of fun.

Antoine the Ant had girlfriends galore,
And cared not how many he hurt,
Then came the day when Annie the Ant
Sent him on his way with a spurt.

Archie the Ant to his rescue came,
To cheer him and make him feel better,
But Antoine was sad and deeply upset,
And wished he had never met her.

The very next day, Archie the Ant
Called on his Romeo friend,
He found him quite jolly, with a new girl called Molly.
"Oh good," said Archie, "he'll mend."

Boris the Bullfrog

Boris the Bullfrog bellowed so loud,
He disturbed everyone on the pond,
His ear ached so much, he'd gone daft in the head,
And each note was like beating a gong.

Boris the Bullfrog was never quite quiet,
He was big with a very large nose,
And when he had earache, everyone knew,
He couldn't lie quiet and doze.

Bazil the Medic came along with a cure,
But had to be sneaky and slick,
He crept silently by on a bullrush leaf,
And slapped on the compress, real quick.

"Blazes," cried Boris, "you've killed me for sure,"
As he clutched at his aching ear.
Then all of a sudden the mists rolled away,
Old Boris was sleeping – what a cure!

Cuthbert the Cuckoo

Cuthbert the Cuckoo sat still on his nest,
Waiting for worms from his mum,
He'd grown bigger and bigger, as each day passed,
There was no satisfying his tum.

His mum was a warbler, so pretty, so gay,
But was gradually getting so thin,
She hadn't the time to feed for herself,
Whilst filling young Cuthbert the bin.

At last came the day when Cuthbert flew,
His mum breathed a sigh of great joy,
She trilled and she flew, way up in the sky,
So proud she had reared that great bouncing boy.

Cuthbert the Cuckoo, so large and so grey,
Sat high on the branch of a tree,
Cuckooing loudly, all the day long,
"I'm Cuthbert the Cuckoo, that's me."

Danny the Dragon

Danny the Dragon puffed and he blew,
Shot out his fiery forked tongue,
He was a dragon, well known far and near
As the dragon who bursts into song.

His ancestors, see, were Welsh, don't you know,
At every Eisteddfod found him there,
Thrilling the crowds with his range of high notes,
Straining his throat without care.

The great day arrived when he should appear,
The crowd getting larger each hour,
Danny the Dragon puffed and he blew,
But he'd lost all his notes, all his power.

Danny the Dragon puffed and he blew,
But he never again sang his song,
He went back to his cave, on the side of the hill,
And just shot out his fiery forked tongue.

Ellie the Elephant

Ellie the Elephant, kindly and large,
Lived in the zoo, with her mother,
She giggled and gushed, trumpeted loud,
Gave rides round the park with her brother.

Ellie the Elephant, kindly and large,
Ate buns the kids handed over,
She stuffed herself silly with apples and pears,
Sat down with a bump in the clover.

Ellie the Elephant, kindly and large,
Hiccupped quite loudly and long,
Gurgled and hiccupped, hiccupped and gurgled,
And ended up with a song.

Ellie the Elephant, kindly and large,
Was spanked by her mother well and truly,
She still gives her rides in the park by the zoo,
She ignores all the tit-bits, and is never unruly.

Fanny the Finch

Fanny the Finch hopped her way through the grasses,
Pecking at each luscious seed.
Oh, how she loved summer, the long sunny days,
She had everything, all she could need.

Fanny the Finch met her old nurse,
By the mill where the stream chattered by,
Her nursey was old and bad on her feet,
But her spirit was willing to try.

Fanny the Finch felt very sad,
To see her old nurse so disturbed,
She passed over her grasses, a box brimming full,
After all, she was such a kind bird.

Gilbert the Gander

Gilbert the Gander ambled along,
Down the long green lane by the church,
He suddenly spied, in a gap in the hedge,
A *fox*! His heart gave a lurch!

Then just as he thought all hope was gone,
The farmer came by with his load.
"Jump aboard," cried he, "land in the hay."
He lived, as the story has told.

Harry the Hippo

I'm Harry the Hippo,
I hump and I haw.
I'm Harry the Hippo,
The one with the jaw.

I'm Harry the Hippo,
I browse in the lake.
I'm Harry the Hippo,
I'm asleep, then awake.

I'm Harry the Hippo,
Trotting on shore.
I'm Harry the Hippo,
The one who's a bore.

I'm Harry the Hippo,
I puff and I blow.
I'm Harry the Hippo,
I'm silly, I know.

Isodore the Iguana

Izzy the Igg was as hard as stone,
Both in body and mind much the same,
From his scaly great head to his pointed great tail,
He lived up to his crazy old name.

Izzy the Igg decided to change,
So he went to a fancy dress ball.
He went as a moth, with gossamer wings,
And won the first prize, best of all.

Izzy the Igg, with his great scaly form,
Flew by on his gossamer wings,
From his scaly great head to his pointed great tail,
He lifts up his voice and he sings.

Johnny the Jackdaw

Johnny the Jackdaw was such a great snob,
From the top of his head to the end of his tail.
He puffed himself out with importance so big,
He fell off his perch with a wail.

He fell with a thud on the ground far below,
Lying stunned, 'neath a large copper beech,
Winded and wounded, his pride all in shreds,
And no one to hear within reach.

He lay all that day, in the hot, burning sun,
Crying and moaning in pain,
But just as night fell, his brother flew by,
Just as it started to rain.

Johnny the Jackdaw was no longer a snob,
His pride had taken a great fall.
And now he is seen, on the branch of the beech,
A friend to each one, one and all.

Katie the Kingfisher

On a bank by the river, a kingfisher sat,
Her plumage so bright and so blue,
She preened and patted her feathers so neat,
And thought, "What on earth can I do?"

Her babies had flown, she'd swept out the nest,
She'd polished it shining and bright,
Then turning her head, on a bough she espied
A youngster, quite trembling with fright.

Katie's concern was painful to see.
"I've lost my Mama," said the sprite,
"I'm wet and I'm cold, hungry as well,
I must look a terrible sight."

Katie enfolded him under her wing,
Dried his eyes with a bright orange feather,
"Come home with me, and we shall have tea,
And talk it all out together."

The youngster stayed on with Katie some time,
But then one sweet day, with the fields full of hay,
His mother came fluttering by.
Oh, how they rejoiced, and oh, how they cried,
And really what more can you say?

Lawrence the Lion

I'm Lawrence the Lion,
I roar and I bawl.
I'm Lawrence the Lion,
The king of them all.

I'm Lawrence the Lion,
With a mane like a rug.
I'm Lawrence the Lion,
With my head on a mug.

I'm Lawrence the Lion,
The jungle's my home.
I'm Lawrence the Lion,
and –
I'm all on my own.

Maisie the Minnie Mouse

Maisie was a minnie mouse,
Maisie was a beauty,
Maisie's fur was soft as silk,
With whiskers strong and tail so long.
Maisie was a minnie mouse,
Maisie was a beauty.

Maisie was a minnie mouse,
Maisie had a boyfriend,
He had fur as soft as silk,
With whiskers long and tail so strong.
Morris was a minnie mouse,
And Morris was a beauty.

Maisie married Morris Mouse,
They were very happy,
They had fur as soft as silk,
With whiskers strong and tails so long.
They had a home and family three,
And all of them had beauty.

Norman the Nuthatch

Norman the Nuthatch wound his way up the tree,
Feasting on tiny green flies,
"Oh, what joy it is to be free,
Flying high to the heavenly skies."

Norman the Nuthatch flew higher and higher,
So overcome was he,
Now he is known as the Nuthatch in Heaven,
Sitting proud on a pearly white tree.

Oswald the Owl

Ossy the Owl tu-whitted, tu-whooed,
Waiting to leave the old barn,
When the moon rose to full, he spread his great wings,
Flew quickly away from the farm.

Ossy the Owl was kindly and wise,
And he knew there was mischief about.
He'd promised his neighbours, Oggy and Onn,
He'd enquire from Konrad the Kraut.

Ossy flew on to the farm on the moor,
Where Konrad was hunting for food.
He found him soon, by the light of the moon,
And challenged him, just where he stood.

Konrad the Kraut was a coward, deep yellow,
And Ossy the Owl knew this well,
He told him to stop poaching their land,
And to be an awfully good fellow.

Ossy the Owl flew back to the farm,
To see his old friends, Oggy and Onn.
"Now we'll be free to hunt over our farm.
Good show, Ossy Owl – well done!

Percy the Pike

Percy the Pike prodded Stickleback Sid,
He was out to annoy him that day.
Percy the Pike was the king of the pond,
And was never loving and gay.

Percy the Pike was old and quite grey,
No one really knew his great age,
He'd lived in the pond, for years so they say,
Getting more and more livid with rage.

Sidney the Stickleback sought out his friend,
Freddie, the handsome young frog.
Together they decided to play him a trick,
And hide away all of his grog.

Percy the Pike wailed loudly with grief,
"I've lost all my whisky and gin,
Please bring it back, I promise I'll change,"
And opened his mouth in a grin.

Percy the Pike prodded Stickleback Sid,
He was out to please him that day.
Percy the Pike was the king of the pond,
And was now always happy and gay.

Queeny the Quail

Queeny the Quail sat on her eggs,
Hidden by gorse and heather,
She was late with her hatching, looked nervously round,
She sensed something wrong – whatever?

Queeny the Quail left her young batch,
To survey the land all about her,
She'd heard in the distance the voice of a man,
Could it be poacher, or keeper?

Queeny the Quail fluttered with joy,
The voice seemed to get fainter and fainter.
"Thank goodness," she cried, "my eggs are now safe,
I shall now have a nap until later."

Reggie the Rat

Reggie the Rat swam along by the bank,
Past the nest where the moorhens sat,
He listened in awe to the willow trees roar,
As the wind blew great gusts through his hat.

His hat he'd acquired on the day before this,
Quite accidently it seems,
It was floating along, on the current mid-stream,
And fulfilled all his wildest dreams.

He'd longed for a hat as jazzy as that,
It was straw, with a great yellow bow.
He tied up the ribbon under his chin,
Set off up the river real slow.

Reggie the Rat swam along by the bank,
Past the nest where the moorhens sat,
He preened and he preened, as everyone gazed
At the bright yellow bow on his hat.

Sidney the Snail

Sidney the Snail was full of great charm,
His manner was gracious and kind,
He lived in a garden, with pathways galore,
And plenty of food to find.

Sidney the Snail had a sweetheart, named Sal,
Who was plain to a painful degree,
But Sidney was blind to the lack of such charm,
And only could say, "*She's* for me."

Sidney the Snail, with his charm and his grace,
Wooed Sal with a garland of flowers,
He trailed round the roses, the pansies and leaves,
But was met by plain Sal with glowers.

Sidney the Snail, with his grace and his charm,
Gave up the fight for plain Sal.
Went on with his life in the garden of flowers,
And soon found a pretty young gal.

Tommy the Tortoise

Tommy the Tortoise trotted along,
His shell shining bright in the sun,
He called on his friend, the mole in the hole,
Intending to have lots of fun.

Poor Moley was sick, with a cold in the head,
His snuffles, heard miles around,
Syrupy stuff on a tray by his bed,
On his neck, a nice woolly was wound.

"So sorry," said Moley. "That's OK," said Tom,
"You'll be better tomorrow, then we'll play.
I'll trot along quick now, before it gets dark,
But tomorrow I'll come, and I'll stay."

Tommy the Tortoise trotted along,
His shell shining bright in the sun,
He called on his friend, the mole in the hole,
And they soon hurried off to have fun.

Unwin the Unicorn

Unwin the Unicorn, gallant and bold,
Stood by the cave in the woods,
He'd called on his pal, Leo the Lion,
As every good friend always should.

Unwin and Leo had fought in the past,
Many battles, which neither had won,
Now they met up on high festive days,
And together, they had lots of fun.

Leo the Lion had a birthday this day,
He's five, perhaps four, but not sure.
Unwin had brought wild strawberries for tea,
And a pot of thick cream, all so pure.

They sat down to tea, with the strawberries and cream,
Brown bread, honey and iced cake.
They ate fit to burst and laughed till they cried,
And everyone said, "What a noise they do make."

Violet the Vixen

Violet the Vixen, pretty as paint,
Her red hair so long and so shiny,
Decided to take a trip to the sea,
And to paddle, down in the briny.

She travelled by train, first class, of course,
After all, it was only one day.
She raced to the beach and was met with a shock,
"What's happened?" she said, "Tell me, pray."

The sea had gone out, disappeared from all view,
The beach was just miles and miles long,
Poor Violet sat down and cried in despair,
"It's all gone so terribly wrong!"

Violet went back to her home, on the train,
Travelling first class, of course.
"Never mind," she said, "I've enjoyed my day out,
Speeding fast on the train – no remorse."

Wally the Walrus

Wally the Walrus swam all day,
In the cave with the silver sand,
A mermaid he knew was poised on a rock,
A comb and a glass in her hand.

Her long golden hair, fanned out in the wind,
Her mirror flashed bright in the sun,
Poor Wally was dazzled, and before he could stop,
Hit the rock like a shot from a gun.

Poor Wally the Walrus lay flat on his back,
With a lump on his head like a pea,
The mermaid swam by, with a laugh and a cry,
Poor Wally was left all at sea.

Xavier the Zyphoid

Xavy the Xyph was a fish with a sword,
He was brave as a knight of old,
He lived in deep water, with his son called X-ray,
And taught him to be true and bold.

Xavy the Xyph was honest and brave,
And guarded his home with care,
He flashed his great sword, polished so bright,
And did somersaults with real flair.

Xavy had battles, was scarred and quite battered,
His life work to guard the weak,
He imagined himself in a coat of gold chain,
And fought so well for the peak.

Xavy the Xyph died in great age,
He was over a hundred years old.
Now they all miss their gold knight errant,
And feel Xavy's story be told.

Xavy the Xyph's friends in the deep
Erected a stone in his name.
It was gold, of course, with a point like a sword,
Recording his glory and fame.

Yolande the Yeti

Yolande the Yeti lived high in the Alps,
Her fur black as coal, and quite rough.
She worked very hard, as all yeti do,
All she wanted was a new powder puff.

Now as you all know, the yeti are shy,
And no one has properly seen them,
They hide behind trees, in the hills and the snow,
Keep very still – then vanish.

Yoris the Yeti, had many ideas,
He wanted to please his Yolande,
So he gathered together all the flowers gone to seed,
And made a great puff for her powder.

Yolande the Yeti cried tears of great joy,
As Yoris presented it to her.
Now she's so pretty, with her new powder puff,
They've decided to marry next summer.

Zoa the Zebra

Zoa the Zebra lived on the veldt,
A black and white striped martinet,
Handsome and bold, with a beautiful head
And a family of five – a quintet.

Zoa the Zebra, who lived on the veldt,
Had a wife, also handsome, called Zelda,
His children all three, Zim, Zak and Zee,
Also one more, called 'the Elder'.

Zoa the Zebra, who lived on the veldt,
Looked after the Elder, called Zam.
Zam was his father, his mother had gone,
Shied, turned one day – and ran.

Zoa the Zebra, who lived on the veldt,
Gave chase, but was never to find.
He returned to the fold, with a heart full of stone,
Lived on years long, with his kind.

Springtime

Springtime, springtime, the joy of it all,
After the winter's darkness and cold.
The snowdrops, the violets, lifting their heads,
Nature's story once more to unfold.

The tulips, the daffodils, waving their heads
To all and sundry passing by.
The flashes of scarlet, yellow and blue
Make us all catch our breath with a sigh.

Summer is near, the birds are all singing,
Springtime is launched with great glee,
The trees spread their boughs, their leaves thick and green,
Warmth and delight are waiting, all for you and me.

Summer

What joy it is in summer,
Watching all the flowers grow.
Banks and banks of vivid colour,
Blues and pinks and yellows glow.

Antirrhinums, phlox and roses,
Gardens full of wasps and bees,
Columbines, 'hocks and pansies,
Dazzled by all one sees.

Live through joy, live through sorrow,
Flowers help us through it all.
Praise to God for all the beauty,
Passing summer to glorious fall.

Autumn

Autumn is here in a blaze of glory,
The leaves, shining in amber and gold,
Covering the paths, the lanes and the landscape,
Winter is nigh with icicles cold.

Bonfires and fireworks celebrate the Fifth,
Halloween and witches, and bumps in the night,
Sparklers glittering in tiny hands,
No one is worried or overcome with fright.

The excitement and flashes are over,
Everyone departs for their homes,
With bags of chestnuts and golden apples,
Bags and baskets are full of groans.

Autumn has faded away into winter,
Christmas and the festivities get near.
The skating and skiing soon fill our dreams,
And expecting it all again next year.

WINTER

Wintertime is fast approaching,
When leaves begin to fall,
The fields of corn are stored away,
The oxen and the horses, safe within their stall.

Flurries of snow, and icy blasts,
Freeze all the blood in your veins.
Blaze up the fire, add some more logs,
Who cares if it blows, who cares if it rains?

Christmas has come, with presents and turkey,
The tree and the crackers are giving such fun,
The children all laughing, with red shiny faces,
Who cares about spring, and the hot summer sun?

The Wild Rose

The wild rose hides in the hedgerow,
Practically hidden from view,
It nods its head in the light summer breeze,
Fills the air with its perfume, too.

The rose only blooms for a very short time,
Engulfing us all with its smell.
For centuries long it has blossomed each year,
Its beauty for all to tell.

The wild rose is pink, and a delicate green,
No artist can capture its beauty,
It nestles deep down with the thyme and the rue,
On a bank, in a hedge, such beauty.

A Dog - A Spaniel Dog

Well beloved! How well beloved a dog can be,
With his long, long lashes and blackcurrant eyes,
How gentle his gaze for all to see,
But most of all for me, how wise.
Well beloved, how well beloved a dog can be.

Nothing

We make such a fuss of the things that we do,
And really, it's nothing.
We make such a fuss of the things that we say,
And really, it's nothing.
We brag and we boast till the end of the day,
And really, it's nothing.
Nothing to do, and nothing to say,
It can't be true, can it?
Not really!

The Tramp

A great brown bundle arose from the hedge,
It moved very slow, with great stealth,
The tramp was emerging, from his temporary bed,
Clutching a carrier, holding all his wealth.

Now summer has come, he could walk the lanes,
With no fear of being cooped up indoors.
The world was his oyster, his own man again,
No more working long hours, scrubbing floors.

He spread out a cloth on the fresh green grass,
Took out his bread and his cheese,
Uncorked his bottle with strong sweet tea,
Ate hearty, and burped. "Oh, manners, please!"

The old tramp walked on for the rest of the day,
At peace with himself and the world.
When sunset was nigh he had supper of rabbit,
Spread out his sack, and into it curled.

The very next day when the sun rose up high,
The great brown bundle did not stir.
The tramp had died in the night, of old age,
Happy, contented and free from all care.

Bubble Bath People

Where are the serious, strong-minded people?
Have they got lost in the rush?
Pushed firmly aside by the power-driven gourmets,
The ones with the cheek and the push.

Where are the beautiful and artistic people?
Are they surrounded with trash?
Trying so hard to lighten the thinking,
In a world that is geared to the gaudy and brash.

The bubble bath people disappear like the foam,
They're really not worth much thought.
They've exploded and gone, like the gust of a wind,
Left behind nothing, at least nothing one sought.

Where are the serious and strong-minded people?
Have they got lost in the rush?
Not on your life, they're quietly proceeding.
Quietly dealing with the cheek and the push.

Old Age

Where do you go when you're old and grey?
What do you do with your time?
How do you get through the chores of the day?
How do you do?

Where do you sleep when you can't climb the stair?
Where do you lay your weary head?
How do you ask for affection to spare?
How do you do?

Somewhere not far is a kindly heart,
Somewhere a soul that is true,
Then, thank God, someone to impart,
How do you do? I do!

Why? (1)

Why do we pray for treasure in heaven?
Why do we long for treasure on earth?
Where are we going, what are we doing?
Working and sleeping, and crying with mirth,
Why are we here?

In heaven, on earth, beauty abounds,
To blot out the horrors of darkness and fear,
Wait for the call, whenever it comes,
Goodbye to all that, that one holds dear,
Why are we here?

Death has a sting, so final, so hard,
When loved ones and friends depart from one's eye,
How can one's soul exchange for such worth,
When we are dead – we shall know –
Why are we here?

Faith must conquer our fears and our woes,
Faith must be foremost, in thought and in deed,
Faith is the answer, our pros and our cons,
Faith is the answer –
Why are we here?

Why? (2)

Wondering why we love you?
Wondering why we care?
Wondering why?
You're just there!

Retirement (1)

Retirement – how strange and how odd,
Leaving behind all of life's work,
Caring and worrying over people and things.
Retirement! – How strange and how odd.

All of the fervour, the battles have gone,
Strange is the silence, left in its wake.
How will I conquer feeling so much?
Get on with it, fool, there's joy to be found.

Joy of life, of loving and giving,
Joy of the world, its goods and its wealth,
Joy most of all of friends and of chatter,
Joy, joy, joy, I'm free at last.

Come to me, life, come and God bless,
All nature's glories, to love and behold.
Out in the sunlight and bask in its rays,
Love life, love people, gaze, gaze and gaze.

Retirement (2)

After the toil, the rush and the hassle,
Peace, quiet, rest and me.
After the joy, the jokes and the laughter,
Peace, quiet, rest and me.

After the worry, the fear and disquiet,
Peace, quiet, rest and me.
After fulfilment in a job well done,
Peace, quiet, rest and me.

The Human Race

How interesting is the human race,
With all its quirks and change of face,
Determined all to cut a dash,
However silly, however rash.

How beautiful can they be?
How wise and clever for all to see,
Gifted, astounding, full of charm,
Dirty, dishevelled and full of harm.

Dustmen, watermen, policeman and crier,
The ambulance men and men of fire,
The nurses, the doctors, lighting the lamp,
The kindness, the sorrow – the vamp.

The children so pretty, so naughty, so bright,
Playing and laughing, a lovely sight.
Crying with mirth and crying in pain,
Over and over, and over again.

The love of one's country, one's home and each other,
Caring and loving, each sister and brother,
Mothers and fathers, uncles and aunts,
Grandparents, both to flaunt.

Loving our pets, hating the weather,
Working and fighting hard to endeavour –
To keep life good and full of grace,
That we can look long, at the human race.

Waiting

Some of us stand in the wings of life,
Raising our eyes to the stars,
Watching the world as it idles along,
Drifting with clouds, thinking of Venus and Mars.

People stare long, gaze on for ever,
Wondering about you and your kind.
You stare back and gaze on for ever,
Imagining what secrets to find.

As some of us stand in the wings of life,
Others go rushing along,
In their hurry, they've missed all the beauty,
And just merge with the everyday throng.

What of others, the don't cares and sluts,
Taking all they can get without trying,
Thank God for the people who stand in the wings,
At least they're not moaning and crying.

Hedgerows

Rainbow colours splash the hedgerows,
Colours of rare and mystic hues,
The pink of the campion, cow parsley white,
The sweet briar rose and periwinkle blues.

The dandelion glows like the sun at noonday,
The hogwort stands tall and proud,
Honeysuckle entwines through the leaves of the ivy,
And the violets and primroses scatter the ground.

Hedgerows in winter are covered in berries,
Berries of orange and berries of red,
Painting the countryside with dark leaves of holly,
Sparkling and glowing in icicles white.

The hedgerows in springtime are a brilliant green,
With pink and white buds awaiting to burst,
The chatter of nestlings and the chorus of birdsong,
The perfumes and breezes enfolding our world.

THE GYPSY

The morning mists enfolded the landscape,
Penetrating every copse and dell,
Soundless and silent it moved through the trees,
Deeper and deeper it rose and fell.

The scent of a fire pierced the nostrils,
Curling its way through the tallest trees,
The Gypsy had come stealthily and quiet,
Not making a sound, not disturbing a breeze.

She camped in a clearing of chestnuts and oaks
Next to a stream of pure clear water.
She set up her tripod and lighted a fire,
Put on her stew as her mother had taught her.

The vardo stood at the edge of the clearing,
Painted in colours of every hue,
Spotless and clean in Romany fashion,
In reds and greens, yellow and blue.

The Gypsy herself wore gold and jewels,
A gay coloured scarf covered her curls,
Curls which were once black as the night,
Now like the fire were wispy furls.

Her family had left her to live out her days,
In the place she loved best of all,
The place where she'd seen the first light of day,
Heard the birds sing and watched the leaves fall.

Now she would die in the same well-loved wood,
With the birdsong, the mists and the rain.
The sun would rise high one morning, one day,
But the Gypsy had gone far, far away.